IT MUST BE TRUE

IT MUST BE TRUE

"It was all in the papers"

by

DENYS PARSONS

✳

Drawings by Ronald Searle ✳

✳

Macdonald
LONDON

Sixth Impression February 1957

First published in 1952 by
Macdonald & Co. (Publishers), Ltd.
16 Maddox Street, W.1
Made and printed in Great Britain by
Purnell and Sons, Ltd.
Paulton (Somerset) and London

INTRODUCTORY NOTE

"If it is a cold day, cut a few slices from your tongue and serve with a brown sauce." It may have been this passage from a cookery book that gave me the urge to start compiling this collection of howlers and misprints from newspapers and books. I am glad to acknowledge my indebtedness to *Punch*, to the *New Yorker*, and to *Breaks* by W. W. Scott (Jonathan Cape, 1931), in which many of them were first published. The remainder are from miscellaneous sources and from my own collection.

When reading a newspaper you may occasionally have been puzzled by a few words of complete gibberish, spliced without warning into the middle of sensible text. As often as not it consists of the magic words ETAOIN, SHRDLU, and CMFWYP. These correspond to the familiar QWERTYUIOP of the typewriter and are the first three columns of keys on the compositor's type-setting machine. If the compositor makes a mistake he cannot correct it; the whole line has to be completed and scrapped. So he just finishes it off in the easiest way by running his left hand down the keys, and starts afresh. The metal castings of these faulty lines are later returned to the melting pot, but occasionally an odd one gets through to the press.

I like to imagine that Shrdlu is a real person, constantly at work behind the scenes to create a new world of fantasy, reaching beyond the literal errors of the compositor, to the *faux pas* of harassed reporters and sub-editors, and the *double-entendres* of inexperienced authors and copy-writers. This then is the story of Shrdlu.

5

Mr. and Mrs. Shrdlu are still living, and at their request I am restricting biographical notes to the barest outline. Fortunately most of their story has been told already in the columns of newspapers and magazines, and I have done no more than select appropriate passages to illustrate the Shrdlus' contribution to the gaiety of nations.

From the earliest days it was clear that the infant Gobfrey,* though not without his glorious moments, was destined for a life of embarrassment, disillusion, frustration, and danger. And the same is true of his wife Lousie,* née Cmfwyp, who was of course of Welsh extraction. For these two even to get born was a perilous adventure. . . .

* Publisher's note. Presumably the compiler means Godfrey and Louise.

7

In our last week's issue we announced the birth of a son to Mr. and Mrs. Gilbert Parkinson. We regret any annoyance that this may have caused.

Indian Paper

This picture shows the "Blizzard Baby" who was born in a hospital parking lot unnoticed by her father and mother, who collapsed as she stepped from an automobile.

American Weekly

Mr. and Mrs. A. P. Hageman are rejoicing over the arrival of a mafwpy cmfwyp emfwpy cmfpwpp doing nicely.

Florida Paper

January 20th, at Kenyon Road, Wavertree, to Mr. and Mrs. Oswald Unsworth, a son (bath well).

Liverpool Echo

Chauffeur-handyman, aged 40; wife Vienna cook; occasionally one child.

Advert. in Morning Paper

Due to an error Mr. and Mrs. S. E. Ankrum, 104 West Healey St., are the parents of a girl, born Tuesday morning in the Mercy Hospital.

Illinois Paper

Katherine Riddell was born at the little village of Peasley. Her mother was living there at the time.

Local Paper

Mrs. George Earl, who gave birth to a 19-year-old daughter is reported as getting along fine. A. J. Dill of Farley, who suffered a broken leg in the same accident, is recovering.

Moran Times, Tennessee

Mrs. David Miller has a new baby boy at her house. Dave is just as happy as if it was his.

Ohio Paper

Gobfrey Shrdlu and Lousie Cmfwyp each spent a turbulent childhood. One memorable summer, when he was twenty and she was seventeen, they met in Fleet Street. It was loev at frist sihgt.

He looked at her with infinite tenderness. "I know all about it" he said.

She covered her face with her hands and cried brokenly. But, coming closer, he put both hands on her shoulders, and lifted her tea-stained face to his.

Tasmanian Courier Annual

"I—I didn't know you cared for me in that way. I've always thought of you as just a great big bother."

Newspaper Serial

"I've something to tell you, Peggy. I may call you Piggy, mayn't I?"

Short Story

He leaned his head against her hair. A wasp strayed across his face. He kissed it.

Novelette

Mary's eyes rested lovingly on the little gold brooch. "Oh, Jack," she murmured, "it's the loveliest gilt I've ever had."

Serial Story

The last he saw of her was as she turned out of a side-street into the main road, tearing up the latter as she went.

Weekly Paper

It is proposed to use this donation for the purchase of new wenches for our park as the present old ones are in a very dilapidated state.

Carrolton (Ohio) Chronicle

*Having decided to get married, Gobfrey and Lousie lost
no time in arranging for the wedding. It would be agreeable
to be able to say that everything went without a hitch, but it
would not be true. Every step was fraught with embarrassment, particularly for the bride and her family.*

The bride, who was given away by her father, wore a dress
of pale bridegroom. She was attended by the hat, and
carried a bouquet, the gift of the pink taffeta silk and a large
dark blue bridegroom's two little nieces.

Kentish Paper

The bride carried a handsome bouquet of harem lilies.
North London Paper

The bridegroom's mother wore pale gray chiffon with V
neck, short sleeves, and skirt having a cascade down the front.
With it she wore Harvard University with the Head of the
division of chemistry, and returned to Cleveland only a few
days ago.

Cleveland Paper

The bride was attended by her sister and Miss —— as
bridesmaids, all being very strongly under the influence of
drink. VERY CHOICE—James Brothers' Coffee.

Birmingham Paper

On Monday Councillor Thomson's son will be married
to the eldest daughter of Councillor James. The members of
the Corporation are invited to the suspicious event.

Suffolk Paper

The bride was dressed in a light place in the Wesley Temple
in Minneapolis, with Dr. James Brankburg, pastor, officiating.

Iowa Paper

11

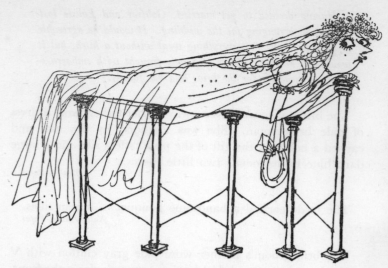

The bride will be supported by five piers.

Evening Standard

Here the couple stood, facing the floral setting and exchanged cows.

California Paper

Appropriate music was played on the organ by Mr. G. E. satin with pearl trimming. Her train was that on earth do dwell" and "Father, now Thy grace extending."

The bride was becomingly attired in white Good. The hymns sung were "All people of silver lace, and she wore a tulle veil, which had been used at her mother's wedding.

Local Paper

The service was conducted by the Rev. ——. After the Benedictine, Mr. and Mrs. —— sang "I'll walk beside you."

Report of Wedding

The bride wore a gown of white sheer with lace insects.

Cleveland Paper

The bridegroom travelled in a two-piece clerical gray angora, striped with red and beige, worn with a black Robin Hood hat, trimmed with red.

Essex Paper

Until further notice, no steam-roller, steam-wagon, heavy lorry, or charabanc, will be allowed to run over the bride.

Bedford Paper

After the honeymoon the Shrdlus began the interminable search for a house and furniture.

FOR SALE—A small bungalow containing five estate agents.

Local Paper

House and shop for sale; excellent position; tenant under notice to expire end of March.

Welsh Paper

Oak bedstead, 3ft. 6in. with wife and wool mattress, new condition, £5 10. 0 lot.

Provincial Paper

One unusual feature is a so-called bachelor's chamber with a private bathroom. The maids' bedrooms and bath are conveniently located and are reached by a private stairway.

Newhaven Journal-Courier

The entire estate, totalling nearly £300,000 has been left for the purpose of building a home for indignant people.

Calgary Albertan

TURKEY CARPET for Sale good condition the property of a lady too large for her rooms.

Advert. in Scotch Daily

In the end the Shrdlus decided to take the first house they had seen advertised. With difficulty they evicted the five estate agents who were squatting there, then moved in and settled down to the humdrum of married life. Perhaps they had more than the usual trouble with the local tradesmen.

BIRTHS, DEATHS, and MIRAGES

National Daily

B—— & Sons, home-decorators and plumbers, etc. All work cheaply and nearly done.

Advert. in Perthshire Paper

The plumbers have finished their part of the contract at the new township, and there now remains only the plumbing to be done.

Australian Paper

The stove will stand by itself anywhere. It omits neither smoke nor smell.

Newcastle Paper

Why rend your garments elsewhere when our up-to-date laundry can do the work more effectively?

New Zealand Paper

He was asked if he contemplated any further act of matrimony.

"Certainly" was his evasive reply.

New York World

We've got fifty Yankettes married into English nobility right now. Some are duchesses. Some are countesses. Eleven are baronesses. Only one is a lady.

Boston Globe

"Yes," she said, "those things over there are my husbands."

Newspaper serial

To bring wives over by telephone without permit, consult Mr. —— , Marine Superintendent and Receiver of Wrecks.

Notice at Naval Base

IRATE HOUSEHOLDERS—Why be swindled in a clumsy manner? Fetch your second-hand clothing to me and be done in the most approved style.

Advert. in Daily Paper

Now that the war is over, may we be allowed to book forward your Spring requirements? Our Mr. Hackett, who has just been disembodied, hopes to call quite shortly.

Tradesman's Circular

Mrs. —— requires useful ladies' maid for town and country; only ex-soldier or sailor need apply.

Provincial Paper

Mr. and Mrs. Wally Burman of Sioux Falls have just arrived at the Lindau home where they will be housepests for several days.

Minnesota Paper

My wife took an instant dislike to my guests and went out of her way to make painful scones.

Evening Paper

Gobfrey will not talk much about his early days in business, and it is uncertain whether he was a commercial traveller or an advertising man. But one thing stands out clearly in all records extant of his transactions—his strict regard for honesty.

RAINCOATS AT LESS THAN COST PRICE LAST THREE DAYS

Advert. in Midlands Paper

Our 'ETERNA' Fountain-pen is a revolting invention.

German pamphlet

OUR LOW PRICES ARE THE DIRECT RESULT OF OUR LOWERED PRICE POLICY

Advert. in New York Times

Should a customer cut his hair and shave at the same time, the price will be one shilling.

Jamaican Daily Gleaner

During the morning there was a steady demand for coarse yarns.

Financial column

NO ICE SOLD AFTER 4 P.M. ESPECIALLY 5 CENT PIECES

Shop sign in Baltimore

CLOTHES BRUSH. The genuine pigskin back opens with a zipper and inside are tweezers, scissors, nail-file, and a bomb.

All our season's Goods will be offered at most treasonable prices

We never allow a dissatisfied customer to leave the premises if we can avoid it. It doesn't pay.

BLANK'S MACARONI AND CHEESE
IN
TOMATO SAUCE
containing
TOMATO SAUCE, MACARONI and CHEESE

Americans are offered perfect Grandfathers, one dwarf, one inlaid.

In the foreign exchange market, the $6.58\frac{1}{2}$ zipT shrdlu shrdlu cmfwyp shrdlu franc was dealt in around 5.12 cents.

Try our patent mosquito destroyer coil, 1s. 6d. It is perfectly safe for mosquitoes.

The young couple were good church-goers. They can hardly be blamed for the awkward incidents that attended their visits to places of worship.

The public is to be allowed to inspect the Crematorium on Sundays. Other amusements will be found advertised in the local Press.

Canadian Paper

The interesting announcement is made that Finchdale Priory has been handed over to the Society for the Prevention of Ancient Monuments.

Provincial Paper

VISIT OF 10 WESLEYAN MINISTERS TO C—— CHURCH

———

"Is happiness possible today?"

Northern Paper

HYMN . . . No. 336
 (Congregation standing)
SERMON, "What are you standing for?"—Dr. Fosdick.

New York Church Bulletin

Owing to the continued illness of the Vicar, which we trust is reaching its last stage, the services have been conducted by the Rev. ——

New Zealand Diocesan Magazine

WESLEYAN CHURCH

Minister: Rev. J. Flesher Rumfitt
11 a.m. Rev. J. F. Rumtt
7.30 p.m. Rev. J. F. Rufimfitt.

South African Paper

The new automatic couplings fitted to the organ will enable Mr. —— to change his combinations without moving his feet.

Parish Magazine

Browsing one day in a second-hand bookshop, Gobfrey picked up a cheap Textbook of Anatomy, and soon he was taking an almost morbid interest in this subject.

Bob guided her to the spinet. He took his spectacles off his beaky nose and invited Mrs. Ransome to admire it.

"It's much smaller than Aunt Bertha's," she said.

Modern Woman

She stood at the foot of the stairs, narrowing her eyes and breathing through her hips.

Saturday Evening Post

In addition to the fine work done by the **Irish** regiments he assured them that many a warm Irish heart beat under a Scottish kilt.

Daily Paper

He sat there quite calmly, a pipe wedged between his lids.

Boys' Paper

If your skin is not liable to be sensitive, rub the arms gently with pumice stone. This will take them right off.

Woman's Paper

DO YOU WANT A PAIR OF GLOVES MADE FROM YOUR OWN SKIN?

Advert. in London Weekly

Joe lifted his eyes quietly a moment to hers then sat down to his coffee. Without opening his mouth again, he finished this, hesitated, arose. . . .

Story in American Magazine

The eminent statistician rubbed his ear thoughtfully and produced a cigarette.

Short Story

In reply to your valued enquiry, we enclose illustrations of Dining Tables of Oak, seating fourteen people with round legs and twelve people with square legs, with prices attached.

The Huntly Express

Lousie Shrdlu spent a good deal of time in the kitchen, though she seems to have profited little from her domestic science course.

WOMAN HURT WHILE COOKING HER HUSBAND'S BREAKFAST IN A HORRIBLE MANNER.

Headline in Texas Paper

For coping with unexpected guests, it is always a good plan to keep a few tons of sardines in the house.

Woman's Paper

QUICKLY MADE SOUP—Required: 4 lbs. fat, $\frac{3}{4}$ lb. caustic soda, 10 ozs. resin, 9 pints of water.

Sunday Paper

SPECIAL TODAY—Stewed teak and potatoes.

Menu in East End Café

A chicken thief was reported active on Wednesday night, and at the Bennett J. Dickerman property a score of fine chickens were taken from the poultry house. The matter was reported at police headquarters and is being investigated.

A chicken pie supper will be served by the Ladies' Aid Society in Centreville parish house on Thursday at 6 o'clock

New Haven Journal-Courier

Never crumble your bread or roll in the soup.

Etiquette Book

Break the eggs carefully into a basin taking care not to break the eggs.

Cookery Book

Lady will exchange clothing, self, little girl, for farm butter, eggs, jam.

Advert. in The Lady

It's a fine scene, denoting "Eat, drink, and be merry, to-morrow we "Eat, drink, and be merry for tomorrow we lose its spontaneous significance.

Liverpool Paper

A new licence, dated August 20, 1941, has been issued authorizing the use in manufacture of food for animals of any Wheat by-product and also of any milled Wheaten substance produced from unmillable wheat. Millers should note that for the purpose of this Licence, 'animals' includes birds, but not cats or dogs.

Ministry of Food Announcement

THERE IS NO SUBSTITUTE FOR OUR COFFEE SO DO NOT TRY IT

OTHERS HAVE TO THEIR SORROW
Advert. in Canadian Paper

My lunch these days consists of a 2d chair in the park and the Daily Mail.

Letter in The Daily Mail

At next Wednesday's children's party it is expected that in two hours 300 children will consume 1,800 sandwiches and 900 fancy cakes, gallons of milk and tea, pounds of butter and a fishfryer, a plumber, a schoolmaster, and a railway inspector.

Yorkshire Gazette

Wash beets very clean, then boil. When done, swim out into a pan of cold water and slip the skins off with the fingers.

Boston Globe

Sport was one of Gobfrey's many interests. His attendance at sporting events was often marked by unusual incidents.

Robinson, who had been auctioned several times by the referee, was ordered off the field.

Sussex Paper

Len Hutton carried his bath through the innings.

Scotch Paper

That hunting and fishing are good in Colorado is shown by the fact that of 100,000 hunters out during the recent game season there were 80,000 killed. This is a record that cannot be equalled in the United States.

Colorado Paper

30,000 pigeons were released filling the air with the flutter of a million wings.

Commentary in a News Film

West End Milliner will make latest fashion hat each month for 18 months for young well-bred greyhound.

Advert. in Daily Paper

R—— had survived three appeals for l.b.w. before the players retired to lynch.

Daily Paper

Round 3.—Both continued to be cautious in the first minuet, but opened up in the second minuet, when both got in good lefts to the head.

Birmingham Paper

Edward Slater broke his arm last week. It was a decided success and many expressed the wish that it might be an annual affair.

American Paper

24

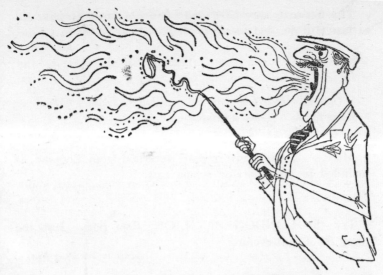

In an interview he said: "I have been all over the world looking for the perfect golf curse, but I think at last I have found it."

Evening Paper

As a matter of fact, Jackson calmly waited to be fetched, and I fear his suffering was not so great as people thought. He dislocated a hip hip hurrah, and was soon all right again.

Provincial Paper

Ten sampans were entered, the boats being gaily decorated with flags. The result was a very amusing race in which the winner passed the post only a length behind the second.

Hongkong Overseas Mail.

I was terrified. . . . There was the tiger crouching, ready to bounce.

Short Story

The forwards shot hard and often but never straight till at last Hill decided to try his head. It came off first time.

Kent Paper

Gobfrey's interest in sport was matched by Lousie's enthusiasm for the world of entertainment.

Miss ——, who only recently returned from England, is included in an otherwise strong cast.

South African Paper

Try the LONDON PAVILION, 8.30 p.m. Just the thing for a dull evening.

Advert. in The Daily News

D—— Amateur Operatic Society. Booing office opens on Monday.

Provincial Paper

NEW YORK, March 4th.—Helen Hayes, whose work on the stage was interrupted by maternity, is to return in a manless play.

Columbus Dispatch

THIS WILL BE A SHOW WHICH YOU MUST NOT FAIL TO MISS.

Advert. in Rangoon Paper

The Ballet travels with its own symphony orchestra which is directed by Mrs. Goberman. The orchestra contains 20 virtuous performers.

Clemson College Tiger

26

In the British Honours List the arts are represented by film actor Laurence Olivier, who receives a knighthood for his services to stage and films, and the same award for services to music went to Dr. Alcolm, a sergeant.

Brazilian Paper

THE BIBLICAL STORY, BASED ON A LIBRETTO BY OSCAR WILDE, RECOUNTS THAT . . .

Associated Press Dispatch

The Concert held in the Good Templars' Hall was a great success. . . . Special thanks are due to the Vicar's daughter, who laboured the whole evening at the piano, which as usual fell upon her.

South African Paper

Miss T—— sang a number of popular ballads while the orchestra played some Strauss waltzes.

Parish Magazine

Mme Albani, it is announced, is going to take a limited number of pupils, but has been sunk. The crew were saved.

North Western Daily Mail

Mme Tetrazzini has not been heard in London for five years and some little ooooooooo aaaaaaaaaaay shd of cwyyyy might have been busy on her voice. Well, it has scarcely.

South African Paper

Wanted for Low Comedian, really funny sons.

The Stage

IT'S THEIR SHOW—Mr. and Mrs. Alvan W. Sulloway, of Concord, N.H., librettist and composer of "Winner Take All". She writes music with her three little boys on her hands.

Boston Globe

Gobfrey Shrdlu fought in more than one war. His shrewd comments on the military situation were not always appreciated by his superior officers.

It is upsetting somewhat the plans of the high German officers who are arranging things from afar through telescopes down which they shout their orders.

Liverpool Daily Post

The officer in command kept his head and cleverly ordered his men to keep behind it as it moved forward.

Daily Paper

PROMOTION. Rifleman P. R. Shand to be Sergeant H. Cock.

Ceylon Paper

Tomorrow week the Canadian regimental doctors will be deposited for safe keeping in Bristol Cathedral.

Bristol Paper

Swooping to a few hundred feet, Nazi planes dropped parachutists onto a narrow plateau, then climbed over a 10ft. wall, and there was Mussolini at an upstairs window.

Belfast Paper

Three later attacks . . . tfoytpop poptpop poptp popt popt yopt . . . were completely broken.

Egyptian Gazette

28

Gen. Graham, who likes to eat as well as any man, would like to see a bit more cor bread ad mustard brees served to the President at the "wite White House" at this aval submari statio.

"Don't get me wrong," he cautioned.

World Telegram and Sun

NO TIME TO WASTE

PRIMATE ON ATOM BOMB

Headlines in Yorks Paper

This week three crows landed at Cardiff who had been sunk by submarines twice, and in some cases three times.

Manchester Guardian

LOOKING FOR THAT SILVER LINING?

You'll find it for sure with the U.S. Army. At no expense, you'll get the finest medical and dental scare.

American Paper

It is up to the regular establishments to institute training programmes that will result in a constant weeding out of those who are found unwilling to or incapable of becoming incompetent.

American Government Circular

M. Leon Blum told a Press Conference in London today that while a prisoner in Germany, he listened to the B.B.C.

"I can't express to you my feelings as each day I heard coming across the air: 'I.C.I. Londres', but it was like a Beethoven symphony."

Leicester Paper

World peace, now as never before, depends for its preservation upon them asses.

Daily Paper

All the six main workships were destroyed, five of them severely.

Daily Paper

The total number of prisoners captured by us in this sector is not yet available. We secured Mayoress, Mrs. Hogg, Mrs. R. Nay, Miss South of the Scarpe.

Provincial Paper

In 1918 he was appointed business manager of the Great War at a salary of £15 per week.

West Country Paper

Soon after he was demobilised, Gobfrey was called to serve on a jury. He was able to make his personal contribution to the annals of crime.

Jenkins, it is claimed, was driving at a high rate of speed and swerving from side to side. As he approached the crossing he started directly towards it and crashed into Miss Miller's rear end which was sticking out into the road about a foot. Luckily she escaped injury and the damage can easily be remedied with a new coat of paint.

Ohio Paper

A full charge of shot struck Mr. Cozad squarely in the back door of the henhouse.

Illinois Paper

P.C. Thomas said he arrested the defendant because his face was beyond the limit fixed for the town.

Manchester Paper

There were two sharp reports, and Radley lunched and staggered.

Short Story

By an unfortunate typographical error we were made to say last week that the retiring Mr. —— was a member of the defective branch of the police force. Of course this should have read: "The detective branch of the police farce."

New Zealand Paper

Referring to Mr. C. T. Williams, the magistrate said: "It's not everyone who has the courage to tickle an armed intruder."

Daily Paper

Policeman Leo Grant was shot through the stomach and John Marcinoak, taxi-cab driver, through the hip, while a trusty at the jail was shot in the excitement.

San Francisco Call-Bulletin

Mrs. Lukes was caught beneath the auto and taken to St. Joseph's Hospital with several fractured bones. The bones were on their way to Woonsocket to spend their holiday.

Connecticut Paper

One of these men, a Calabrian named Motta, went to his partner's shop and tried to shoot him while he was engaged in shaving a customer. The bullet shaved the face of a boy who was waiting.

Egyptian Gazette

Erwen was a man of keen observation. There was something in his visitor's eyes which puzzled him. Suddenly he realized what it was. It was the whisky and soda which he had set down untasted at the corner of the table.

From a Serial by E. Phillips Oppenheim

She could not say on which side of the road he was riding in Commissioner Street, but he turned into West Street on the wrong side. She was sure that after the accident she fell onto the pavement on the correct side of the road.

Johannesburg Star

Rather late in life the Shrdlus had their first child, a little boy who was christened Wil£iam Etaoin. The lad's infancy and childhood were blighted by much the same misfortunes which had dogged his parents.

"If you ask me," said Doris, "it's more like *twelve* years they have been married. I don't think they will ever have a chill now."

Short Story

Mrs. Edgar Ramsden was rushed to Roanoke Hospital on Monday of this week for observation and treatment prior to becoming an expectant mother.

Virginia Paper

When the baby is done drinking it must be unscrewed and laid in a cool place under a tap. If the baby does not thrive on fresh milk it should be boiled.

Women's Magazine

Our morality rate in Fairfield is low while our birthrate is high.

Alabama Paper

Plastic makes a new space saver for mothers who live in crowded quarters or who must travel with a small baby in the form of an inflatable bathtub.

Dallas Morning News

Be sure to keep your children away from this poison. This may not kill them at once but gradually they will all die.

Farming Paper

P. T. Harris gained credit for himself and for Wellingborough Grammar School by passing in every subject and gaining four distinctions—in arithmetic, French, algebra, and Little Bowden Pig Club.

Market Harborough Advertiser

A party from the Grammar School, Ilkeston, of nineteen girls, fourteen boys, two mistresses of one master, leave for an eight days' tour of Paris.

The Ilkeston Pioneer

His mother died when he was seven years old, while his father lived to be nearly a centurion.

Wallasey and Wirral Chronicle

Wrap poison bottles in sandpaper and fasten with scotch tape or a rubber band. If there are children in the house, lock them in a small metal box.

Philadelphia Record

After many years persecution, and twelve children, Mrs. Leah Elkin, Brooklyn, finally graduated from high school.

Kansas City Star

Shrdlu, whose policy of honest dealing had made him a surprising amount of money in business, was determined that his children should pursue higher aims. The eldest boy, Wil£iam Etaoin, was put in for Medicine. Young Timo⅝ȯthy, who was always playing around with valves and Geiger counters, would be a scientist. Let us first see the world through Wil£iam's eyes.

It wasn't the proper doctor—just a young locust taking his place while he was away.

Short Story in The Evening News

Headaches? Let us examine your eyes and help you in removing same.

Notice in Optician's Window

TEETH EXTRACTED WITH THE GREATEST PAINS

Dentist's Advertisement

"The nurses who have a seven minutes' walk to their home quarters, have never had a rude word addressed to them," said the matron, "not even," she added, "when they have had too much to drink."

Daily Province, Vancouver

36

Dr. W. T. —— read an interesting paper on "Idiots from Birth". There were over two hundred present.

Surrey Paper

In the preliminary examination of patients the author introduces a test that is new to us; two or three breaths having been drawn through the nose, this organ is then punched by the anaesthetist, whilst the patient holds his breath as long as possible.

The Practitioner

The increase in number and percentage of autopsies is a tribute to the energy and zeal of the hospital staff in general and to the geniality and personal charm of our chief resident Dr. George Grainer.

Annual Report of a Connecticut Hospital

On making enquiries at the Hospital this afternoon, we learn that the deceased is as well as can be expected.

Jersey Evening Post

Mrs. —— wishes to thank the nurse and doctor for their kind co-operation in the loss of her husband.

North Bucks Times

The seaman, severely injured when the ship was three hours out, was taken to hospital and the hippopotamus removed.

Daily Telegraph

Timothy Shrdlu's scientific training taught him to think clearly and logically.

Recent tests conducted by a zoologist prove that grasshoppers hear with their legs. In all cases the insects hopped when a tuning fork was sounded nearby. There was no reaction to this stimulus, however, when the insects' legs had been removed.

Corning Glass Works Magazine

Lamps must be long enough to be efficient, and the average length is likely to increase. Prolonged deliberation at one laboratory has produced the following rule on maximum lamp length: "No lamp shall be longer than the maximum dimension of the room it is intended to fit."

Electrical Engineering

Valve Triste (Sibelius).

Wireless Programme

The use of salt for snow clearing after an experiment on Friday, was discontinued, because (a) it was too snow was do deep it melted the cold (the weather), and (b) the salt instead of vice versa. So shovel gangs continued to remove it the old-fashioned way.

Montreal Paper

"If it is not worth while going on with the race it is not worth while going on with the race it is not worth while going on with the race," commented Dr. Saleeby.

Manchester Evening Chronicle

All the chemical elements are dissolved in sea-water. The explanation is that rivers have been carrying dissolved miners into the sea for millions of years.

Oregon Paper

COUNTLESS OTHER WORLDS

Dr. Jones's argument for believing that there are countless other worlds where living beings are present, briefly, is this:

Ninety per cent of the shrimps served on the tables of the United States come from the coastal waters of Alabama, Florida, Georgia, Louisiana, Mississipi, and Texas.

Mineapolis Tribune

YOU CAN SKATE MORE THAN ONE MILE ON ONE SLICE OF BREAD

Saturday Evening Post

Before its late summer departure the sparrow will build several nests and will bear many little sparrows, judging from past performances.

Mrs. Hetherington said that she had not had the same luck with male birds.

The Sun

Dr. Brode told the reporters he was "not very impressed with the chances of obtaining 'atomic powers' out of cosmetic rays."

New York Times

SIR WILLIAM RAMSAY'S POSER STARTLES AUDIENCE

London, February 4th. Sir William Ramsay raised the question whether the unfit should be left to die at the annual dinner of the Institute of Sanitary Engineers tonight.

Montreal Gazette

Letters were sent to 665 men. Each envelope was marked "Important" in large letters, so that those men who could not read might ask to have the letters read to them.

American Education Digest

We make a speciality of gorillas and chimpanzees. They are wonderfully intelligent and can be trained right up to the human standard in all except speech. One of our directors, Mr. —— and his wife are both able to be tamed to live in captivity.

Irish Paper

TOTAL ECLIPSE OF THE SUN

L.M.S. RAILWAY COMPANY'S ENTERPRISE

Dorset Paper

He had the privilege also of viewing a number of rare
Egyptian tummies.

Cleveland (Ohio) Paper

Electrocution of microbes is the latest dental method. The apparatus consists mainly of a violet ray, a glass tube, and an insulted sofa.

Canadian Paper

Zoologists could only visit the hot springs in El Hamma with the permission of the local Kaliphat and with an escort of police, since it is reserved for the exclusive use of Muslim women bathers. An attempt was made to bring back a number of specimens alive in vacuum flasks so that further investigation could be carried out in Oxford.

Illustrated London News

As a sideline Timothy made money as a consultant to the Quiz editors of several newspapers.

Q. What is the derivation and meaning of the name Erwin?
A. It is English from the Anglo-Saxon and means Tarriff Act of 1909.

Columbus Citizen

Q. How may slightly soiled playing cards be cleaned?
A. They are made by stringing pieces of meat, quarters of onions, and two-inch pieces of bacon on sticks and broiling them over coals.

American Magazine

Thirty thousand feet is a great height for aircraft. Forty thousand feet, to which it is said the Messerschmitt 109F can get, is greater.

Sunday Paper

The age limit for Girl Guides was formerly 18 years, but by general request it has now been raised to 81 years.

Morning Paper

To repair damaged tablecloths, first lay the tablecloth flat, with the hole uppermost.

Dublin Evening Mail

WORDS OFTEN MISUSED: Do not say: "We then drove over the bride." Say: "We then drove across the bride."

Union City Hudson Dispatch

Q. How can you tell the age of a snake?
A. It is extremely difficult to tell the age of a snake unless you know exactly when it was born.

Detroit News

The Librarian reports that we now have in our Reference Library a larger number of boobs than has any other library in the County.

West Country Paper

SAY IT RIGHT

Today's names in the news and how to pronounce them:
Syngman Rhee, President of Korea; pronounced Sung-mahn Ree.
Jacques Fath, French fashion designer; pronounced Ellsa Skee-ah-pah-rell-ee.

Miami Daily News

*At about this time a small fire at the Shrdlu shrdlu cmfwyp
shrdl eeeeoetaoin small fire at the Shrdlu home caused Gobfrey
to ruminate about fires in general.*

The faces of the two men were livid with rage as she
quietly crumpled them up and threw them on the fire.

Short Story

Colonel Marsden says that the fire was a terrible blow to
him for he had spent a large sum of money on it and had
extensions and improvements in view.

Yorks Paper

All the goods saved from the ruins was a bushel of potatoes.
They escaped only in their night clothing.

Pennsylvania Paper

The Brigade was called and distinguished the flames.

Evening Paper

The Chairman said the Council had never paid one penny
for the oiling and washing of the Fire Brigade.

Local Paper

The Lomas Fire Brigade was soon on the scene and helped
by members of the railway personnel were able to reduce the
two carriages to a smouldering heap.

Buenos Aires Herald.

The fire, which started at 8.30 a.m., was extinguished after
six hours fight. It is thought that combustion was the cause
of the fire.

Illinwis Paper

With the children off their hands Gobfrey and Lousie Shrdlu could devote more time to their garden and smallholding.

Send mother a gift of hardly ever blooming rose bushes.

Sioux Falls Argus-Leader

Mr. —— held that purchased meat should be better than that supplied by contractors, who were not saints. He knew of one case where cattle were actually killed after they died.

Irish Times

Dig the ground over thoroughly and then pant.

Gardening Article

It was one of those perfect June nights that so seldom occur except in August.

Magazine Story

STOCKINGS DOWN AGAIN
WANTED: FAT CALVES

Adverts. in Jersey Paper

Practise thinning in winter time and head back in summer. A tree can be kept bearing practically regular crops. Of course it is impossible to keep any tree bearing practically regular crops, but of course it is impossible to keep any tree bearing a full crop regularly. Wonders can be done by this system of pruning.

Nurseryman's Leaflet

WANTED—A steady young woman to wash, iron, and milk two cows.

New Zealand Paper

Keen educated young woman wants Agriculture or part Agriculture and Secretarial work in Blandford area. Three months' farm experience, good shorthorn typist.

Advert. in West Country Paper

The first few days the chicks were fed inside the brooder house on pieces of asbestos concrete sheets, 3 ft. long by 2ft. wide.

Poultry Article

Different colours of the same variety of flowers will usually blend well. But just let three or four plants of magenta sweet williams show up near three or four pale pink petunias and WoW!O)?!$§/. following?

California Paper

A sample of milk from a churn was found to contain added water to the extent of $6\frac{1}{2}$ per cent. Milk taken direct from the cow was genuine.

Essex Paper

Another new Order stated that a farmer may slaughter his own household on condition that seven days' notice is given to the Food Committee.

Provincial Paper

"Wild Foods of Great Britain" with 46 figs. 1s. 6d. nett.

Times Literary Supplement

TOO LATE FOR CLASSIFICATION—12 March and April pullets laying rabbits.

Advert. in Local Paper

Not long ago they decided to hang the expense and take their first real holiday abroad. Naturally there were endless discussions of the relative merits of travel by air, sea, road, or rail.

Among the first to enter was Mrs. Clara Adams of Erie, Pa., lone woman passenger. Slowly her nose was turned around to face in a south-westerly direction. Then like some strange beast, she crawled along the grass.

California Paper

5-seater car for sale; must sell; chauffeur at the Front; own body cost over £73. What offers? RECTOR.

Advert. in The Times

He could see a dim red tail-light about a mile ahead of him. Oliver switched off his own lights and rammed down the accelerator with clenched teeth.

Short Story

There is apparently very little fear on the part of the travelling public that their inconvenience will be seriously interfered with.

Birmingham Paper

BOMBAY—The English Mail Steamer was signalled this morning at 5.20 and is expected to arrive at the Central Post Office, Calcutta, by special train tomorrow night.

Calcutta Paper

Altrenhein, Switzerland—Bucking wisps of snow and bitterly cold wind, the DO-X took off from Lake Constance this forenoon for a six hour fliflgflhfltflfltflofl.

Boston Traveller

She proceeded on her way until 7, or rather later, when a noise was heard as of a heavy body like an anchor or a chain being dragged along the deck from about the funnel aft. It was the mate's watch.

Liverpool Paper

As architect and builder of all the property in these roads, I am in a position to say that they are in every way perfectly bbbbbbbb.

Local Paper

The motorist stuck miles from anywhere has only himself to blame if he has not brought an up-to-date road mop.

Weekly Pictorial

Most of the owner-drivers I know make a practice of washing their ears at least once a week.

Motoring Paper

Three hundred emigrants arrived here today by train, 90 per cent of them being people of both sexes.

Irish Paper

In many other towns the trolley buses are virtually silent. Surely it is not beyond the ingenuity and industry of Birmingham to stop the awful screech ours make as the conductor runs along the overhead wire.

Letter in the Birmingham Mail

48

The skipper spat disconsolately down the engine-room ventilator and stopped the engines.

Sea Story

After their holiday the Shrdlus felt strong enough to face once more the inevitable discomforts and tribulations of domestic life. In their turn WilƐiam and Ti⅝ⓦmothy had by this time braved the dangers of a Shrdlu courtship and wedding, so, I am glad to say, there is no danger of the race dying out.

Mrs. Joe Sexton and children, of Deadwood Gulch, were guests of the A. Dennys family on Sunday.

Mrs. Dennys is almost confined to her bed with nervous exhaustion.

Lady wishes to exchange from 15th July to 15th September, young Englishman for young Frenchman.

RA RA RA RA . . . Mrs. J. P. Reynolds is confined to her home on Tilney Avenue with illness.

Nobody ever shouted "Good old Albert" to the bearded husband of Victoria, but plenty of people have shouted it to the easy-going debonair Philip.

LOST. Friday night between Market Square and Dimsdale Avenue, Black and White Terrier. Name and address on collar of owner.

Double-action Gothic Harp (by Erard), suitable for a lady in perfect condition.

While your partner is dealing the cards you should be snuffling.

Daily Paper

Mrs. Alice McCrory and son, Harvey, went to Dayton last Sunday to visit Mr. and Mrs. Carl Dunbar, who were slightly injured in an automobile accident last week. Mrs. Dunbar before her accident was Miss Olivia McCrory.

Ohio Paper

LOST, Fri. night, between Oughtibridge and Hillsboro', a small red-faced Lady's Wrist-watch; sentimental value.

Sheffield Star

DELTA, Colorado. When Mrs. A. S. Glassiter, 82, died recently she on a basis of the acreage planted, was survived by her husband, 13 bushels less than the normal yield children, 80 grandchildren and 25 great-grandchildren.

Staten Island Advance

On Wednesday evening Mr. R—— proposes to take the life of one of the modern poets.

Durham Paper

Lady wishes to travel in exquisite lingerie.

Daily Paper

WANTED—a good cook; kitchen-maid kept; small fairy.

Provincial Paper

Dover—Gas up 5d. a 1,000.
Tunbridge Wells—Gas up 2d. a 1,000.
Lord Selborne up again after a chill.

Evening News

The will disposes of a million-dollar estate, the bunk going to relatives.

Washington Star

At a Texas port the largest wooden ship ever built has been launched just five months after the keel was laid. She is fitted with tripe expansion engines of 1,450 horse-power.

Yorkshire Evening Post

Before sailing for Egypt John spent a few days in Dorset and no doubt then wrote the verses entitled: "Somewhere in England" and beginning:

EFFECTS OF RHEUMATISM

Dorset County Chronicle

Information wanted as to the whereabouts of Mrs. J. O. Plonk (Blonk) wife of J. O. Plonk (Clonk).

Advert. in Chinese Paper

It is scandalous to see these Society women going about with a poodle dog on the end of a string where a baby would be more fitting.

New Zealand Paper

Mr. Asquith was accompanied by Mrs. Asquith and the audience singing "For he's a jolly good Lady Bonham-Carter".

Scottish Paper

A PRETTY KNITTING PATTERN

Cast on any to serve:—To each pound of carrot pulp number of stitches that can be divided by five; 1st row Knit 1.

Northampton Daily Chronicle

Its lone peal summons the faithful to worship while the others are dismantled and repaired.

Bucks Advertiser

PARISIAN BEHEADED FOR KILLING
WIFE BEFORE MISTRESS

St. Louis Post-Dispatch

On this distressing note we take leave of the Shrdlu family.
They would greatly prefer to retire into obscurity, but their
public will not permit it. Even now a thousand newspaper
men are concocting the latest items of gossip and information
about their doings.

And tomorrow I, the grateful chronicler, will begin with
scissors and paste to compile a new book. If any reader
should spot the Shrdlus at work in his daily reading he is
cordially invited to contribute.

RONALD SEARLE

has also illustrated

London—So Help Me!

by

WINIFRED ELLIS

So you plan to settle down in some nice, cosy and inexpensive " digs " in London; somewhere quiet but fairly central so that you can both get to work and enjoy the pleasures of The Town without wasting time, money or energy. Well, we wouldn't say that Miss Ellis wants to discourage you, to make your flesh creep as it were; BUT there are one or two little things she would like to explain to you in advance. Railway porters and private hotels, service flatlets and taxi-drivers, the ways and whimsies of the London bus; these are among the targets of this very funny book.

"Astringent Searle and delighting and delightful Ellis."—*Manchester Evening News.*

" Will be enjoyed by all save possibly the landlords and landladies of Divan Service Flatlets."—ALAN MELVILLE (*B.B.C. Light Programme*).

Crown 8vo.   *4s. 6d.*

_____

MACDONALD & CO. (Publishers) LTD.
16 MADDOX STREET, LONDON, W.1